THE HANDBOOK OF NEW
PARADIGM RESEARCH

THE HANDBOOK OF NEW PARADIGM RESEARCH

THE LASZLO INSTITUTE OF NEW PARADIGM
RESEARCH

Printed in the United States of America

First Printing, 2018

ISBN-13: 978-1-945390-25-8 print edition
ISBN-13: 978-1-945390-26-5 ebook edition

Waterside Press
2055 Oxford Ave
Cardiff, CA 92007
www.waterside.com

CONTENTS

FOREWORD

An Institute dedicated to research on what it calls the "new paradigm" is morally as well as intellectually obliged to say what it means by this term. It is morally obliged to do so, because claiming that its work is of relevance to today's world, it invites people to take notice of it, and if so motivated, to join it. And it is intellectually obliged because work on the new paradigm calls for collaboration with like-minded people to develop its tenets and applications. This Handbook is the Institute's response to the challenge of meeting these obligations.

What do we mean by new paradigm? Einstein noted that scientists seek the simplest possible scheme that can tie together the observed facts. By new paradigm we mean the simplest possible scheme that can tie together the facts brought forward by the diverse disciplines concerned with our observation and understanding of the world.

Developing such a scheme is a meaningful, indeed, an essentially important project. The range of observed facts has been growing exponentially in recent years, and schemes that could tie them together have received scant attention. We have paradigms in physics and in biology, in psychology and in the social sciences, but we do not have a paradigm that would tie together the claims and findings of these discipline-bound fragmentary paradigms. Consequently we lack the insight and the overview that only an encompassing paradigm can provide.

The new paradigm must be encompassing, but it need not and must not repose on personal insight alone. It must be sourced in the facts reported by the discipline-bound paradigms, and thus have a reliable basis in science. Yet that paradigm cannot be a mere integration of these facts. A paradigm is a fundamental view of the world, and when it is consistent, that view is reflected in the interpretation of all the facts on which it reposes.

Philosophers have noted that observations do not themselves determine the meaning attached to them: every observation is capable of a variety of interpretations. In deciding the best interpretation to attach to the facts, science is guided by the ideals of simplicity and comprehensiveness. The new-paradigm scheme must be as simple as possible—but not, as Einstein also said, simpler. It must be as comprehensive as possible, tying together all of the facts relevant to its aims and concerns.

Seeking such a scheme is an ambitious, but not a quixotic, endeavor. The world around us is not a random assembly of unrelated things and events—its coherence, as nearly all great thinkers and scientists in recent times have affirmed, is among its most astonishing features. Searching for this coherence and building on it to gain a sound understanding of the world is a legitimate task of science and science-minded philosophy. It is the task of elaborating an optimally simple comprehensive scheme to account for the facts, the scheme we call the new paradigm.

The first Part of this Handbook outlines the principal features of the comprehensive yet optimally simple scheme that makes up the new paradigm. Its fundamental postulates respond to three perennial queries: *where have we come from? where are we going?* and *who are we?* The second Part elaborates the relevance of the scheme to the major fields and disciplines of the contemporary world: the sciences of life, medicine and healing, education, politics, economics, and business.

This undertaking is ambitious and inherently feasible, but it is not and cannot be dogmatic. Certainty is reserved for the theorems of logic and mathematics; statements become uncertain to the extent that they refer to the real world. Such statements, Plato said, are but likely stories. Hence this assessment of the new paradigm does not aspire to certainty, but it does aspire to be a basis for the likeliest story we can now tell. The task of the Institute of New Paradigm Research is to research, elaborate, and articulate that story. This is basic research in the truest sense of the term, and it is necessarily interdisciplinary: it builds on facts and findings coming from a variety of fields and disciplines.

The publication of this Handbook is an invitation to the reader to collaborate in the elaboration of the new paradigm, and in the exploration of its application to the principal fields of scientific and human interest.

Ervin Laszlo
September 2017

* * *

PART I.

THREE PREMISES OF THE NEW PARADIGM

1. ORIGINS

(Where We Come From)

A new paradigm for our thinking about the world emerges in the assessment and integration of the revolutionary findings that come to light at the frontiers of contemporary science. In light of these findings, the world is very different from that maintained in classical physics. It is not the arena of bits of matter moving in passive space and indifferently flowing time. As astrophysicist James Jeans noted over a hundred years ago, the world is more like a big thought than like a big rock.

The concept of a thought-like world is familiar from the history of thought. Philosophers, scientists, and intuitive people in all walks of life have always questioned that the world would be as it is presented to our senses. Their doubts were well founded: the picture of the world emerging in the contemporary sciences differs fundamentally from the world-picture even of classical physics. The world is not an ensemble of separate bits of matter obeying mechanistic laws; nor is it an arena for the motion of matter in passive space and indifferently flowing time. The world as we come to know it is an intrinsically whole super-quantum system, where all things are connected beyond the hitherto recognized bounds of space and time.

The new concept the world accounts for the origins of the things we encounter around us. It accounts for the origins of the world, and for our own origins. We, as all things, are sets and clusters of vibration originating and persisting in the universe. These vibrations are ordered: they are highly, indeed staggeringly, *coherent*. To use a term suggested by David Bohm, the vibrations that constitute the reality of the world are "in-formed"—they are, non-accidentally, and perhaps intentionally, "formed."

In one form or another, the concept of the world as vibration has been known and affirmed in the great wisdom traditions. It was present in the Sanskrit concept of Akasha, and was taken up in the Vedic texts of India as early as 5,000 BCE. In the *Vedas* its function was identified with *shabda*, the first vibration, the first ripple that constitutes the universe, and also with *spanda*, the "vibration/movement of consciousness." The contemporary Indian scholar I.K. Taimni wrote:

> There is … a mysterious integrated state of vibration from which all possible kinds of vibrations can be derived by a process of differentiation. That is called *N.da* in Sanskrit. It is a vibration in a medium … which may be translated as "space" in English. But … it is not mere empty space but space which, though apparently empty, contains within itself an infinite amount of potential energy … This infinite potentiality for producing vibrations of different kinds in any intensity or amount is due to the fact that at the back of Akasha, or hidden within it, is consciousness.[1]

This formerly esoteric notion is now sustained and elaborated at the cutting edge of physics and cosmology. Research on the ultra-small dimensions of the world reveals that space

---

[1] Taimni, I. K., *Man, God and the Universe*. Madras: The Theosophical Society, 1969.

is not empty and smooth, but filled with waves and vibrations. At the sub-quantum dimension, physicists do not find anything they could identify as matter. What they find are standing and propagating waves—clusters of stationary and propagating vibration.

Previously scientists assumed that it is matter that vibrates. There is a ground-substance that vibrates, and that substance consists of matter-particles and assemblies of matter-particles. The world is material, and vibration is the way matter behaves. But the contrary turned out to be the case. There is no ground-substance. The world is a set of variously formed clusters of vibration, and matter is the way the vibrations appear on observation.

Max Planck said it clearly. In one of his last lectures in Florence, he noted, "As a man who has devoted his whole life to the most clear-headed science, to the study of matter, I can tell you as a result of my research about atoms this much: There is no matter as such. All matter originates and exists only by virtue of a force which brings the particles of an atom to vibration and holds this most minute solar system of the atom together."[2]

Planck was not alone in stating the concept of the world as force and vibration. Two years prior to Planck's pronouncement, Nicola Tesla said that if you want to know the secrets of the universe, think in terms of energy, frequency, and vibration.

The materialist concept of the world has run its course. The new physics tells us that it is not from bits of matter but from clusters of highly ordered "in-formed" vibration that the things we find in the world are built. The in-formation of the vibrations

---

[2] *Das Wesen der Materie* [The Nature of Matter], speech in Florence, Italy, 1944. Archiv zur Geschichte der Max Planck Gesellschaft, Abt. Va, Rep. 11 Planck, Nr. 1797.

makes the world what it is: a system of coherent clusters and waves of vibration, and not a welter of random things and events.

The affirmation, "the world is in-formed vibration" begs a further question. If the world is vibration, what is it the vibration of? What is it that vibrates? It could not be a material substance, for we have no independent evidence for the existence of such a substance. It could not be the known fields either: the properties of these fields have been meticulously mapped, and they do not explain the reality of the phenomena that constitute the world. But the question is badly posed: it suggests the classical subject-predicate concept of physical reality. It asks for the subject of the predicate "vibration." There is no such subject: in-formed clusters of vibration are not vibrations "of" anything. They are themselves the reality of the world.

We can situate the vibrations in the context of what we already know about the universe. The vibrations that furnish the universe appear in the excited state of the wider reality we call cosmos. The singularity known as the Big Bang excited the cosmic ground-state and brought it into vibration. That was the origin of our world. The phenomena we encounter in this world are the vibrations of the excited ground-state of the cosmos.

The vibrations that resulted from the in-formation of the cosmic ground-state have been spatially as well as temporally related. They introduced space and time into the undifferentiated wholeness of the ground-state. The world we know is the cosmic domain created by spatially and temporally related vibrations.

The vibrations and the clusters and sets of vibrations that make up the world are spatially and temporally related, and they are complex and differentiated. They are not random phenomena but the effect of what we can consider the "in-formation" of the universe by the deeper reality of the cosmos. This in-formation is continuous and seamless. There is no empty space and passive time in the world. As quantum physicists recognize, space is filled with fields and forces; it is a foaming, turbulent medium. The term "vacuum" does not apply to it: it is a *plenum*. There are no passive intervals in the plenum—there is no unit of time without dynamic process.

The observed and in principle observable facet of the world is the ensemble of the vibrations resulting from the excitation of the cosmic ground-state. Everything we perceive and know as the real world is a phenomenon produced by the in-formation of clusters of vibration in the spacetime region we call universe. The perceived and perceivable phenomena range in size and complexity from quarks and quanta to living organisms, and from biospheres and planets to galaxies and the metagalaxy. In their ensemble, the in-formed vibrations of the cosmic ground-state produced the physical phenomena of the universe. The world, ourselves included, originated in the excitation of the cosmic ground-state, and it exists and evolves as clusters of in-formed vibration. These clusters appear to human observers as various kinds of physical entities, as living organisms and systems of organisms, and as the integration of all these things in the cosmic spacetime domain we call universe.

Consequently the query, "where we come from" has a new answer. We come from the excitation of the ground-state of the cosmos, and we are an integral part of the excited cosmic ground-state—of the universe.

＊＊＊

2. EVOLUTION

(Where We Are Headed)

1
3.8 billion years before our time, the Big Bang brought forth ripples in the fundamental domain that was primordially the undifferentiated ground-state of the cosmos. This event marked the origins of the world, including our own origins. The ripples evolved, and their evolution yielded hints as to where they are headed. The quantum particles that make up the ripples have been undergoing a nonlinear yet overall unidirectional process of structuration. This process is what we call evolution in the largest, cosmological sense. It defines to where we, and all other things, are headed in space and time.

Since the work of Darwin and Wallace, evolution has been recognized as a process of progressive change in the living world. But what would have produced this change has not been established. Philosopher Henri Bergson postulated an *elan vital* that counters the trend toward the degradation of energy in living systems, and biologist Hans Driesch called for a counter-entropic drive in nature he termed *entelechy*. Teilhard de Chardin and Erich Jantsch invoked the notion of *syntony*, and other investigators spoke of *syntropy* as the force behind the evolution of living organisms.

Since the latter part of the 20th century, evolution has been recognized as a universal process, taking place not just in this biosphere, but throughout the universe. It originated when the Big Bang created Planck-scale disturbances—"ripples"—in the primordial Minkowski vacuum. Particles such as *leptons* (electrons, muons, tau particles, neutrinos), *mesons* (pions), and *hadrons* (baryons including protons and neutrons) were catalyzed, and they radiated throughout the expanding spacetime of the new-born universe. They acquired structure and coherence. They clustered into atoms, and atoms clustered into molecules and molecular assemblies. On the astronomical scale stars, stellar systems and galaxies had formed.

As already noted, the things originating in the excitation of the ground-state of the cosmos proved to be extraordinarily coherent. This coherence characterizes the universe itself. Already in the middle of the 20th century Arthur Eddington and Paul Dirac noted unexplained "coincidences" in the relations between the universe's basic parameters. The ratio of the electric force to the gravitational force was known to be approximately 10^{40}, and the ratio of the size of the universe to the size of elementary particles turned out to be about 10^{40} as well. This is surprising, since the ratio of the electric force to the gravitational force should be unchanging (these forces are constant), whereas the ratio of the size of the universe to the size of elementary particles should be changing (given that the universe is expanding). In his "large number hypothesis," Dirac speculated that the agreement between these ratios, one variable the other not, is more than mere coincidence. But if so, either the universe is not expanding, or the force of gravitation varies proportionately to its expansion.

More recently Menas Kafatos showed that many of the ratios among the parameters of the universe can be interpreted on the one hand in terms of the relationship between the masses of elementary particles and the total number of nucleons, and on the other in reference to the relationship between the gravitational constant, the charge of the electron, Planck's constant, and the speed of light.

The mass of elementary particles, the number of particles, and the forces between them display harmonic ratios. Moreover, the microwave background radiation—believed to be the remnant of the Big Bang—turned out to be astonishingly coherent: it is dominated by a large peak followed by smaller harmonic peaks. The series of peaks ends at the longest wavelength Lee Smolin termed R. When R is divided by the speed of light we get the length of time independent estimates show is the age of the universe. When we divide in turn the speed of light by R (c/R), we get a frequency that equates to one cycle over the age of the universe. And when R is squared and divided by the speed of light (R^2/C) we get the measure of acceleration in the expansion of the galaxies.

The universe's parameters are precisely correlated: variations of the order of one-billionth of the value of some physical constants (such as the mass of elementary particles, the speed of light, the rate of expansion of galaxies, and two dozen others) would have resulted in a universe without stable atoms and stable interaction among them. Even a minute variation of some of the basic physical constants would have precluded the evolution of life. The universe proved to be a coherent system, with parameters finely tuned together and consistent with its overall dimensions.

Not only is the universe highly coherent in itself; it is also the template for the evolution of highly coherent systems. The systems that emerge in the course of evolution display intrinsic as well as extrinsic coherence. Intrinsic coherence means that all parts of the systems are interconnected, with every part responsive to, and aligned with, every other part. Extrinsic coherence means that intrinsically coherent systems are coherently related to other systems around them. Intrinsically as well as extrinsically coherent system are said to be supercoherent.

It is entirely improbable that coherent systems would have come about by a random mixing of their constituents. Randomness, even if encompassing a large number of systems over large time-scales, cannot account for the observations: the search-space of the constituents even of relatively simple systems is so vast that random trial-and-error would have exceeded the available time frames. There were up to 13.8 billion years available for the evolution of atoms and other basic physical entities, and more than four billion for the evolution of living organisms—at least on this planet. This span of time, although enormous, is insufficient to explain the evolution of coherent systems through random interactions. The probability that even simple organisms would have come about through a random shuffling of their parts is negligible. The DNA-mRNA-tRNA-rRNA transcription and translation system is complex and precise; it is unlikely that living organisms based on this system would have evolved through a chance assembly of their genetic pool. To produce the DNA of the common fruit-fly by a random mixing of its molecules would require more time than had elapsed since the birth of the universe. And according to mathematical physicist Fred Hoyle, the probability that new species would emerge through a chance mutation of their genetic code is comparable to the probability that a hurricane blowing through a scrapyard assembles a working airplane.

Living systems are extraordinarily complex and coherent. The human body, for example, is made up of 10^{14} cells, and each cell produces 10,000 bio-electro-chemical reactions every second. Every twenty-four hours 10^{12} cells die and are replaced. Molecules, cells, and organ-systems resonate at the same or at compatible frequencies and interact at various speeds, ranging from the slow (among hormones and peripheral nerve fibers), to the very high (along the Ranvier rings of myelin-shielded nerves). The interactions are precisely correlated, involving quantum-type "entanglements" in addition to classical physical-biological interactions.

If random interactions cannot account for the coherence we find in the world, we need to recognize the presence of an ordering factor in evolution. Neither the processes of life, nor the planets on which such processes unfold, could have come about through a series of "coincidences." Beyond serendipity, precise laws of nature appear to be governing the interactions that produce the complex and coherent systems we observe, and also exemplify.

The evolution of life on Earth has been ascribed to a set of serendipitous circumstances. The position of our planet in this region of the galaxy is extraordinarily fortunate but, as it turned out, it is not entirely exceptional. Earth is a planet in the so-called "Goldilocks Zone," neither too far nor too close to its sun, a main-sequence G2 dwarf star.[3] It has the right atmosphere and the right amount of water for producing and sustaining life. It has the right mass and it occupies a nearly circular orbit. It has an oxygen/nitrogen rich atmosphere, and a moderate rate of rotation. There is liquid water on its surface, and a correct ratio between water and landmass. Its surface temperature fluctuates within the narrow range required for life. It is also at the right distance from the center of the galaxy, and is protected from asteroids by giant gas planets. In this position the Sun's heliosphere protects its surface from cosmic rays and pressures lethal for biological systems,

---

[3] This term refers to the fairy tale of Goldilocks and the three bears. Goldilocks found the house of the three bears and in their absence tried the porridge and the beds and discovered that some are too hot or too big, and others too small and too cold. Finally she found those that are just right—like Earth did in the Milky Way galaxy.

and its own magnetosphere protects it from dangerously high energies emanating from the Sun's heliosphere.

Recent findings indicate that the felicitous position of Earth is not truly extraordinary and rare. Astronomers searching with the Kepler space telescope detected several thousand stars that could have planets in the life-friendly Goldilocks zone. More than 2,000 "exoplanets" have been already identified, and many more are likely to be found. On the average, each star in the Milky Way galaxy has at least one planet, and one in five Sun-like stars may have an Earth-size planet in the Goldilocks zone. With 200 billion stars in this galaxy, there could be 11 billion Goldilocks-zone Earth-size planets in the Milky Way galaxy alone—and there are an estimated 10^{22} to 10^{24} galaxies in the universe. Earth is not merely a serendipitous aberration in the evolution of astronomical bodies in this part of the universe.

The roots of life are already present in the physical evolution of the universe; life on Earth is due to more than a series of serendipitous coincidences. Organic molecules, the basic elements of life, are synthesized under a wide range of physical and thermal conditions. A team of astrophysicists headed by Sun Kwok and Yong Zhang at the University of Hong Kong found 130 macromolecules present in the vicinity even of active stars. They include glycine, an amino acid, and ethylene glycol, the compound associated with the formation of the sugar molecules necessary for life. Their presence around active stars suggests that they were ejected in the course of the stars' thermal and chemical evolution.

Organic molecules were discovered in interstellar clouds as well. The incidence of the most complex of these molecules, isopropyl cyanide, has been reported in 2014 by a team of researchers headed by Arnaud Belloche at the Max Planck Institute for Radio Astronomy. Its branching carbon structure is similar to that of the amino acids that form the basis of proteins on this planet.

Further evidence that the evolution of life is not merely due to fortunate circumstances came with the discovery that primordial DNA self-creates spontaneously. The spontaneous self-assembly of DNA fragments a few nanometers in length into liquid crystals drives the formation of chemical bonds and creates chains of DNA. The self-organizing properties of DNA-like molecular fragments over billions of years may have produced the first DNA-like molecular chains on Earth, the same as on other planets. The physics and chemistry of the universe are finely tuned to the evolution of life. Random interactions are supplemented and replaced by interactions precisely coordinated for producing coherent structures.

There must be more to the evolution of complex and coherent systems than a series of happy coincidences. But the mainstream science community is loath to give up the concept of random interactions, fearing that postulating an ordering factor in nature would entail the assumption of a higher design or intelligence present in nature. Physicist Nassim Haramein noted,

> The fundamental axioms and basic assumptions at the root of physical theories ... presume that evolutionary systems emerge from random interactions initiated by a single "miraculous" event providing all of the appropriate conditions to produce our current observable universe, and our state of existence in it. This event, typically described as a "Big Bang," astonishingly is thought to have produced all of the forces and constants of physical law and eventually biological interactions under random functions.[4]

Notwithstanding the concerns of mainstream scientists, the fact that there is more than chance underlying the evolution of coherent systems is becoming clear. There appears to be a factor

---

[4] Nassim Haramein, in Ervin Laszlo, *What Is Reality?* Select Books, New York, 2016.

in nature that makes the evolution of complex and coherent systems lawful, although not mechanistically predetermined. This factor is best seen as a set of instructions for the behavior of particles and systems of particles. In science, these instructions are considered the laws of nature. They bias the randomness that would otherwise reign in the interaction of particles and systems of particles. The ensemble of the known laws of nature is such that they lead to the emergence of complex and coherent systems. In regard to their effect in the world in the course of time, they are algorithms for the constructions of coherent systems.

One of the most basic of these algorithms is the Pauli Exclusion Principle. The principle states that no two electrons orbiting the nucleus of an atom can be at the same quantum state at the same time. Electrons entering the gravitational zone of the nucleus are excluded from orbits that are already occupied and are shifted into free orbits, filling up the energy shells that surround the nucleus. Due to their exclusion, the particles captured by the gravitational field of the nucleus create a complex structure. As a result, the universe is not a heap or conglomeration of an assortment of particles, but a complex structure formed by the spatial and temporal relations of a highly coordinated set of particles.

Atoms are complex and coherent clusters of vibration, and they bond into the still more complex clusters we know as molecules and crystals. Molecules bond in turn in multi-molecular physical-chemical structures, and these are templates for the formation of yet more complex and coherent systems, including those we call living. There is a consistent if nonlinear progression in nature from level to level of structure and organization.

The processes of evolution conduce toward highly coherent systems that maintain themselves in a physically improbable state far from chemical and thermal equilibrium. Evolution, it appears, tends toward bringing forth such systems.

The trend toward coherent systems is clearly evident in the evolution of living systems. Biological evolution, it now appears, optimizes the coherence of living species and is not uniquely oriented toward the Darwinian concept of fitness to the environment. If the Darwinian concept were the goal of evolution, the biosphere would be populated by blue-green algae, amoebae, and other unicellular, colonial, and simple multi-cellular organisms. Many of these species achieved a near-perfect fit to their ecological niche, and nothing short of volcanic eruptions, sudden climatic change and natural catastrophe can lead to their extinction. If fitness were the goal of evolution in the biosphere, these species would have spread and would dominate the web of life. Other than for the occasional mutation that happened to hit on a more complex state of fitness, simple species would be the dominant, and perhaps the only, species in the biosphere.

However, the biosphere is not populated mainly by super-fit simple organisms. Species and populations have often evolved beyond optimum fitness to their milieu. So-called extremophiles explored such unlikely niches as active volcanos, deserts, and the deep sea. They invaded all niches that could possibly support them, and developed resistance to pressures and temperatures that would be lethal to most other species.

The goal of biological evolution, the same as of evolution on all levels of size and complexity, is not to optimize the fitness of systems to their environment. It is to create systems of intrinsic and extrinsic coherence: systems that tend toward the realization of the ideal state best described as supercoherence.

If evolution on this planet is any indication of evolution in the wide reaches of the universe, and if evolution in the universe sets forth its observed course, we obtain an indication of the nature of the goal that underlies its processes. Given that the evolution of life is a part and an expression of the processes of evolution in the universe, and that the evolution of human life is a part and an expression of the evolution of life, where we are going as a species can be defined in reference to the ideal state that underlies all forms of evolution in space and time. If we do not arbitrarily deviate from our course, we would be moving toward higher and higher and higher levels of coherence: intrinsic coherence in our organism, and extrinsic coherence with other organisms, with the biosphere, and ultimately with the whole of the universe.

***

3. CONSCIOUSNESS

(Who We Are)

The universe is coherent, and the systems that emerge in it evolve toward progressively higher levels of coherence. These processes call for a complex and reliable flow of information between the systems and their environment. In more evolved systems, this flow is articulated and controlled by an evolved brain and nervous system. The relevant features of the environment are displayed for evolved systems in the form of brain-transmitted sensations, images, thoughts, and intuitions. Called "consciousness," this display is a vital factor in the existence of complex and coherent systems on Earth, and presumably wherever there is life in the universe.

An articulate form of awareness of their surroundings is essential for the persistence of evolved organisms such as the human. But the articulate form of awareness we know as our consciousness may be more than an instrument of survival: consciousness could be a basic element of the universe.

This formerly "spiritual" assumption is now supported at the leading edge of the natural sciences. As we noted, the universe is not just physical in the classical, materialist sense; it is a highly "in-formed" vibrational domain. The in-formation of physical entities—clusters of vibration—suggests the presence of something that calls to mind consciousness or intelligence. That consciousness or intelligence in-forms the nucleus of the atom, it in-forms the formation of galaxies, and it in-forms living organisms. It endows the entities that display it with identity.

The intelligence that in-forms complex systems is a kind of internal display of the relations of the systems to the rest of the world. On the human level we know that display as our consciousness. It is not necessarily limited to information conveyed by our bodily senses. Beyond producing signals that orient us in our environment, our consciousness could include elements of the intelligence that in-forms us, as it in-forms all clusters of vibration in the universe.

The idea that consciousness is a basic element in the world is not new: it is as old as speculation about the nature of life and mind. It is supported by important observations and experiments. These suggest that "my" consciousness is not created by my brain, any more than a television program displayed by my TV set would be created by my TV set. The same as a television receiver, the brain does not *produce* what it displays: it *conveys* it. If so, then what it displays can also exist beyond the brain.

This conclusion recalls the idea of an immortal soul, a basic feature of religious and spiritual systems. Scientists and other modern people do not subscribe to it. They believe that reality is confined solely to material bodies. Consciousness is not material, they point out, therefore it cannot be real. It can only be a by-product of a material system, namely the brain.

On first sight, the materialist concept of consciousness makes good sense. However, on a deeper look it encounters vexing problems. How could a material brain give rise to a stream of immaterial sensations? How could anything material produce anything immaterial? In modern consciousness research this is known as the "hard problem." It has no reasonable answer. As researchers often point out, we do not have the slightest idea how "matter" could produce "mind." One is a measurable entity with properties such as hardness, extension, force and the like, and the other is an ineffable sensation without definite location in space and an ephemeral presence in time.

However, if consciousness is not produced but only displayed by the brain, we do not face the problem of a material system producing an immaterial flow of sensations. We have a receiver—the brain—that displays information that exists beyond its physical-physiological bounds. The clusters of vibration that populate the world are "in-formed," implying that there is information in the world that does not depend on a receiver to exist. Human consciousness could include elements that are more than the decodings of sensory signals.

The minimally speculative hypothesis is that the clusters of vibration that populate the universe are not uniquely physical in nature: they have a physical as well as a mental aspect. Viewed from the outside, every entity in the universe is a cluster of vibration. But viewed from the inside—from the perspective of the given cluster—it is a perception, an awareness, a "feeling" of the rest of the world. This internal, seemingly subjective but real aspect is not likely to have emerged in the course of evolution; it must have been present when evolution took off in the aftermath of the Big Bang. It was there, and is still there, in every quantum, in every atom, and in every system built of quanta and atoms. Every such entity is a physical entity viewed from the outside; and a mental entity—a feeling, a reception, a display, of the rest of the universe—from the inside.

In some form and level of actualization, consciousness must be present in all clusters of vibration, from quanta to galaxies; it is not limited to clusters with a complex brain and nervous system. Both *physis* and *psyche* are catalyzed in the interaction of clusters of vibration with the world around them.

Consciousness is a fundamental element of the world, but it is not a separate, radically "other" element. It is present in all things in space and time. How such a universal presence can obtain is explained by the holographic principle. As we know, a hologram contains all the information that generates the image at every point of the holographic film or medium, and every retrieval of information retrieves all the information that generates the image. Thus, the most likely explanation of the universal presence of consciousness is that it is holographically coded. Consciousness is a real element of the real world, but it is not coded "in" space and time. It is a hologram coded beyond the spacetime domain of the universe.

The above affirmation is consistent with a much-discussed hypothesis in cosmological physics: the holographic universe theory. Observations, and calculations based on the observations, indicate that phenomena in the *volume* of the universe display information that corresponds to codes at the *periphery* of the universe. This suggests that the observable universe may be a projection of holographic codes at its periphery—or perhaps in another universe.

The holographic principle accounts for the presence of all the information that "forms" entities and processes in every entity and every process. Evidently, a given entity does not display all the information that is active in the universe, only the segment that corresponds to its position in space and time. The rest of the in-formation is implicit, however, in the segment displayed. The articulation and scope of the actual display corresponds to the level of evolution of a given entity. Highly evolved entities display more of the in-formation than simple, less evolved entities. They have a more articulate consciousness.

We human beings are relatively evolved entities—evolved clusters of vibration. As all complex and coherent clusters, we are in-formed by the totality of the in-formation in the universe, but we display only a fraction of that in-formation in our consciousness. That fraction is, however, wrought with significance.

It contains in potential all the in-formation that "forms" the universe.

The sights and sounds, textures, odors, and tastes conveyed by our bodily senses are but part of the information that appears in our consciousness. There are images and intuitions, experiences and feeling-tones that do not originate with the bodily senses. Transpersonal psychologists and psychiatrists call these elements "transcendental."[5]

The transcendental elements of our consciousness come to light at the fringes of our everyday awareness, but they are the substance of the experiences that surface in altered states of consciousness. They appear in the context of traumatic, uplifting, or otherwise life-transforming events. As near-death experiences (NDEs) show, such experiences occur when the everyday operations of the brain are impaired or shut down. This finding makes perfect sense. When the sensory inputs of the brain are impaired, reduced, or cancelled, the non-sensory "transcendental" inputs become more evident.[6]

The receipt and processing of transcendental elements of experience are among the hallmarks of an evolved consciousness. Repeated observations show that as consciousness evolves, it becomes increasingly transparent to its beyond-spacetime origins. It displays a deep connection, even empathy, with people and things both near and far. This hallmark of evolved consciousness

---

[5] See Stanislav Grof, *Psychology of the Future*. Albany, SUNY Press, 2000.

[6] Repeated observations and experiments show that non-ordinary experiences occur primarily when the brain operates in a low frequency range, in the domain of Delta and Theta waves. The frequency of EEG (electroencephalograph) waves in these domains ranges from near-zero to 7 Hertz, whereas the everyday operations of the brain occur in the Beta domain of 12.5 to 30 Hertz and in highly stimulated states reach the Gamma region of 30 to 100 Hertz.

has been reported by many scientists, philosophers, and spiritual thinkers. It has been affirmed in modern times. William James claimed that we with our individual selves are like islands in the sea—separate on the surface but connected in the deep. Einstein said that our separateness is a kind of optical illusion, and Carl Jung claimed that consciousness is part of the *unus mundus,* the universe's single generative and creative principle. Chimpanzee intelligence researcher Jane Goodall affirmed that her life in the jungle taught her that nature and herself are a single consciousness,[7] and physicist Erwin Schrödinger declared that in the final count all mind is one. "To divide or multiply consciousness is something meaningless [he wrote]. In all the world, there is no kind of framework within which we can find consciousness in the plural; this is simply something we construct because of the spatial-temporal plurality of individuals, but it is a false construction … In truth, there is only one mind."

There is a further element we need to add to this review of the principal features of consciousness in the universe. The holographic in-formation of the clusters of vibration that constitute real entities not only *reveals* the oneness of those vibrations, but *creates* that oneness. Evolution forges connection and coherence within and among the clusters. It brings compatible clusters together at various levels of size and complexity, ranging from quanta to atoms, from atoms to multi-atomic molecular structures, from physical-chemical structures to biological systems, and from species and populations of biological systems to embracing bio- and eco-spheres.

If we are to account for the observed facts, we need to recognize an element in the "in-formation" of clusters of vibration in the universe that introduces goal-orientation into their evolution.

---

[7] Jane Goodall, *Foreword* to *The Intelligence of the Cosmos* (2017).

The mainstream concept cannot explain goal-orientation in the universe: it sees the laws of nature as the conveyors of information, as instructions for the behavior of entities and the unfolding of processes. In that conception the laws of nature function analogously to the laws of chess: they are rules that define the "permissible moves." In the physical world, the rules are the laws that define how quanta and systems of quanta can behave under particular conditions. This leaves aims and purposes out of consideration. It states the rules, but not how they are combined and sequenced to achieve particular ends. That purposive organizing factor is not negligible, however: in chess, it is what differentiates the game of the beginner from the game of the grand master. In nature, it is what differentiates a universe that blindly follows the interactions that the laws of nature permit, from a universe that evolves in a comprehensible (even if not pre-determined) manner.

In chess, the "missing factor" is the intelligence of the player in sequencing the moves so as to achieve the purpose of the game, which is to mate the opponent. In nature, that factor is the intelligence that combines and sequences interactions in nature in ways that favor the emergence of coherent systems.

The missing factor in nature is what classical philosophers recognized as the goal or purpose inherent in nature: *Telos*. Modern science resists admitting *Telos* in the world, since it suggests an intelligence that would guide or orient natural processes. The new paradigm, on the other hand, recognizes that factor: it is the intelligence that in-forms the universe. The cosmic intelligence is goal-oriented: it introduces a bias in evolutionary processes toward the creation of coherently related, in-themselves coherent systems.

Although resisted by mainstream scientists, many leading thinkers recognized the presence of an intelligence—a mind or spirit—in the world. Einstein wrote, "Everyone who is seriously involved in the pursuit of science becomes convinced that a spirit is manifest in the laws of the Universe—a spirit vastly superior to that of man."[8] Max Planck said that even the existence of atoms argues for the presence of an intelligent mind. Behind the order we find in the nuclei of atoms, he said, "we must assume the existence of a conscious and intelligent mind."[9] Conventionally thinking scientists do not make this assumption; they dismiss the hypothesis of goal-directed evolution as mere speculation. Yet we now realize that the most plausible hypothesis—the likeliest story Plato said our ideas about reality are at best—is the presence of a *Telos* that orients our evolution, as it orients evolution throughout the universe. This makes us, systems possessing a conscious mind, into naturally goal-seeking entities, co-evolving with other such entities in the spacetime domain we call universe.

∗ ∗ ∗

---

[8] This statement by Einstein was contained in a letter he wrote in 1936 in his native German. It is important to realize that the German word "Geist" has a meaning wider than "spirit": it also stands for mind and intellect. Einstein is likely to have intended that a mind or intellect is manifest in the laws of the Universe.

[9] Planck, as cited above.

PART II.
APPLICATIONS OF THE NEW PARADIGM

INTRODUCTION

The basic premises of the new paradigm hold comprehensive and comprehensible meaning for the conduct of human affairs. They offer guidance for thought and behavior on the premise that human beings, human society, and the human world in general are not separate realities. They developed out of natural processes in the evolution of life, just as life evolved out of natural processes in the evolution of the universe. A human world founded on arbitrary or misguided premises cannot offer an environment in which people can manifest their highest natures, aiming toward empathy and solidarity with one another and respect and harmony with nature.

The contours of society must fit snugly around the shape of reality—that is, the design of society must be in harmony with the true nature of reality for human potential to be unlocked and for positive outcomes to ensue. New paradigm principles, when applied in the world, would allow and encourage human beings to lead creative, enriching, consciousness-elevating lives. Such humans would evolve their environment further still, leading to more coherent social systems, which again would produce 'better' (more coherent and evolved) citizens, in a positively escalating loop.

How major spheres of the human world would shape up if they operated on new paradigm premises are among the critical questions confronting new paradigm research. In this introductory

note, three premises are selected as indications of the direction
this research might take.

*(1) Consciousness is the fount of all 'things'. Immaterial causes
in-form material outcomes. All phenomena emanate from a core
of consciousness.*

This simple premise, when applied and lived, would effect
a revolution in the orientation of health, politics, economics,
business, and education. Considerations of the evolution of consciousness would become ground zero considerations.

With regard to disease processes, symptoms would not be
confused with first causes; treating the spiritual source of every
ailment would be the main priority of the *medical* field (rather
than covering up symptoms with Band-Aids).

In the field of *politics*, this would imply passing laws that
optimize the possibility of consciousness development for all
citizens, based on the understanding that moral order is a prerequisite to freedom, which is a prerequisite for the growth of
consciousness.

In the realm of *economics*, this would mean acknowledg-
ing that society and nature are not externalities, but rather basic
factors in creative processes. And it would mean valuing and
making place for the engines of creativity—those sacred spaces
(impervious to the assault of numbers) where pure thought and
feeling can take place and hence where real creativity can ensue.

In the realm of *business*, applying the new-paradigm premises would mean harmonizing the metrics of outward achievement with real value creation—individual and societal growth
and evolution—so that rewards are commensurate with the general elevating of consciousness. Under such a framework, the
first priority of businesses is to 'brand' their identity and purpose,
and trade in the currency of evolutionary value.

Education, the fruits of which need to infuse and pervade all
other spheres, would be focused on 'spiritual development'—that

is, on nurturing coherence within and among societies via the evolution of consciousness toward love and oneness. Its primary function would be to provide students with an *orientation* to (ultimate) reality—to orient students' thoughts, feelings and lives toward the emerging paradigm of reality. Education for evolving consciousness would be the starting point and destination of every curriculum, the bedrock of every discipline. In the realm of technology, for instance, conscious evolution would keep pace with, and ideally outstrip, technological evolution, ensuring that technology is adding to, and not detracting from, the total of human freedom and the capacity for human growth.

(2) Everything is a manifestation of a Oneness—of a single, all-pervading consciousness—and hence all phenomena are interconnected/entangled/distributed.

This premise has profound implications for various spheres of the human world. *Medical* professionals would more easily see and acknowledge that spirit, brain and body are one, and that the various 'brains' themselves—in the head, heart and gut—are centers of intelligence that operate as a single distributed network.

Such a premise would have noteworthy consequences for the functioning of *political and economic systems.* It would lead to more networked, collaborative approaches to political and business leadership—supplanting notions of combative bipartisan politics and zero-sum economic competition. Capital would be seen as the circulatory system of the social body, connecting human beings in relationships of service and in light of principles of universal validity.

Technology businesses would reflect their new understanding of reality in their products—such as a hyper-distributed, collaboration-facilitating, purpose-affirming internet—serving not only as engines of transaction, but also as platforms that further democracy and deliberation, freedom of thought and action, and mutually responsive connectedness.

The new attitude to *education*—fostering respect, love and empathy for diverse cultures and life forms—would reverberate throughout the other spheres.

(3) The in-formation of the world is nonrandom, evolving toward coherence and empathic oneness. The forces in-forming matter and mind are fundamentally unitary and teleological. Our highest aim lies in aligning ourselves with these forces and being in step with the vector of evolution as it comes to expression in the human world.

This premise, taken to heart, would attune the social sciences to our collective destiny and move us to aid and promote evolutionary processes. It would fundamentally shift the *health* sector's goal from ensuring absence of disease to nurturing and facilitating wellness in body and mind, inspiring a perpetual pursuit of increasingly higher levels of consciousness. For *politics and economics*, accepting this premise would mean being vigilant that civilization is indeed ascending, achieving real progress, increasing its general level of consciousness (and devising the appropriate barometers to gauge such increase). This would translate into feelings of responsibility for creating an environment hospitable to the evolution of all—which would impact decisions around military conflict, climate change, and various other issues. It would imply the speedy, proactive stymying and neutering of the violent, destabilizing pockets of lower consciousness that surface from time to time—largely by assimilating the positive qualities of these negative movements and thus rendering them redundant.

For *business enterprises*, this retuning would mean a new-found awareness of the role of public as well as private enterprises in leading the journey of human and social evolution. Purpose-maximizing businesses stand today at the vanguard of progress. For better or worse, they are the primary vehicles of values-transmission, having supplanted in this regard the tribe, the church, and the modern nation-state.

The principle of coherence-oriented evolutionary development requires that *education* entail not merely the cramming of siloed knowledge and disconnected bits of information, but the pursuit of a cohesive and comprehensive understanding of the nature of reality—a pursuit that transcends the classroom and translates into a lifelong search for true wisdom and its embodied application. It also mandates instilling an awareness of the differing levels of consciousness informing the evolution of our biological and social systems (which a misguided liberalism has rendered 'politically incorrect' in recent times), and a championing of the task that is common to all of them: increasing the consciousness of the evolving systems in the interest of the community of living systems on this planet.

THE NEW PARADIGM IN THE SCIENCES OF LIFE

The facts of living systems are as real and significant as the physical facts studied by mainstream natural science. In the living world, too, forms resolve into forces and vibrations, movements are governed by universal principles, and outcomes are determined by the direction and intensity of the energies applied. Only the forces and energies are of living conscious beings, and their direction is determined by vital urges, emotional motives, mental intentions and spiritual values as well as by physical factors. The contagious nature of vital sensations such as fear, laughter, anger and joy is due to their vibratory character. The power of these vibrations to act instantly over long physical distances is because proximity in life is determined by the vital or emotional intensity of the focus on consciousness of an object, rather than by physical parameters. The same is true of vibrations that give rise to the phenomena of mind and consciousness. .

The tendency in Western natural science has been to dismiss as mere chance or fortuitous coincidence events whose random occurrence is highly improbable, but which lend themselves to rational explanation according to principles of a science of life known to past civilizations and perceptive individuals, but ignored or dismissed by contemporary old-paradigm science. What scientists actually mean by categorizing these events as chance or coincidence is simply that they have not discovered all the factors that are moving events and the principles that govern such movements and do not possess the appropriate instruments to detect and measure their complex interactions. The term "chance" should rightly be reserved for phenomena that are truly random, rather than for those that simply exceed our present understanding and capacity to study.

These observations compel us to reconsider our conception of the evolution of life and consciousness and to consider the probability that life and consciousness are inherent original properties of the domain of vibrations we call the universe. They are only able to manifest themselves under suitable circumstances and conditions, just as the capacity for athletic prowess, artistic skill and genius remain latent until the appropriate internal and external conditions arise for their expression.

We need to reconsider the principles and processes and processes of biological evolution. The premise derived from Darwin's hypothesis is not the only possible or plausible premise. Darwin made two fundamental contributions to evolutionary biology. First, he observed the evolutionary progression of biological forms. Second, he postulated the principle of natural selection as the driving force for that progression. Science has subsequently identified the genetic mechanism for transmission of biological characteristics and has accepted natural selection as the only logical explanation for evolutionary progression. This conclusion is based on the unquestioned assumption that only material factors subject to physical forces and random variation are at work. But what happens if the underlying assumption is not correct?

Phenomena of matter as we observe them through our senses and instruments appear to lack the two fundamental characteristics of conscious living beings. The phenomena appear to be insensible to stimuli and incapable of any conscious or subconscious, voluntary or involuntary response to them. But the principles of life and consciousness may be inherent properties of the in-formation that governs the domain we call universe. These principles are not manifested under the assumptions of physics but are readily apparent in the phenomena studied by biologists and social scientists.

Matter and life are phenomena generated by clusters of vibration in space and time. With this premise of the new paradigm, the evolutionary progression of biological forms can be readily explained as the progressive manifestation and expression of a basic evolutionary principle, present in the "in-formation" of clusters of vibration in the universe. The evolution of the vibrations that give us the phenomena of consciousness provides the impetus and direction for the evolution of biological forms that give progressively fuller expression to the in-formation inherent in the universe, just as the seed contains concealed within itself the potential and impetus for development of the roots, stalk, leaves, flowers, fruits and future seeds. This hypothesis is consistent with the basic features of our observation of nature.

Since Einstein discovered the formula for the interconversion of matter and energy, Western science has been striving for a monism based on the principle that the underlying reality is material force. Its basic premise even today is that all living processes, all forms of consciousness and psychological experiences, are reducible to material forces. In the East, Vedanta also arrived at a monism, but it did so based on an alternative premise. It postulated and confirmed by experience that this universal Force, which is observed by scientists as physical energy and force is only the most visible, tangible expression of a triply-formulated force which also expresses as the vital energy and force of life and the mental energy and force of thought. It further concluded that all three are expressions of a more fundamental force whose essential character is consciousness. The force governing the development of matter, life and mind is a conscious force, though not mentally conscious in the manner of human mentality. It is a universal consciousness that is the source and energy acting subconsciously in the clusters of vibration that manifest the phenomena of matter, and with increasing consciousness as life rises in the scale of consciousness. It is this force that in-forms the energy which gives rise to material forms, subconscious life forms, and mentally conscious forms of thinking in human beings.[10]

Life in the physical body is the energetic medium through which the physical body transmits its sensations to the conscious and subconscious mind and through which the mind transmits back impulses for action to the body. But it is not only that. Life is also a universal force and field of forces in which myriad vibrations flow back and forth between forms and beings. Outcomes are determined by the quality and intensity of the vibrations exchanged as precisely as the outcomes in a cyclotron are governed by the mathematical formula of quantum physicists. Life is a property of individual beings and bodies as studied by the biologist and physicist, but it is no more confined to the physical form or separable from the life in other forms than is the energy of an electron separate, limited and definable in terms of a specific point in space and time, separate and distinct from the territorial reach of all other electrons or limited to a purely physical exchange of forces, as the phenomena of non-locality indicate. Life is a field in which vibrations are exchanged, just as society is a field for the exchange of social and cultural vibrations and influences, which continuously influence each of its members both consciously and subconsciously. These fields are manifestations of the in-formation of the universe by the intelligence of the cosmos—more exactly, by the intelligence that <u>is</u> the cosmos.

---

[10] Sri Aurobindo, *The Life Divine*, p.14

This perspective differs markedly from the purely physical and conventional view of life as a property of each individual biological form, distinct and separable from that of every other form, or the conventional view that every human heart and mind is distinct and separable from that of every other heart and mind. The notion of society as a group of separate individuals affirms only one side of the truth. It fails to take into account the power of conscious and subconscious relationship which makes even the most individualistic society more than the sum of its parts, and even the most individualistic individuals a product and inseparable portion of the wider society in which they live. All are receiving and transmission stations for universal vibrations whose individual character and uniqueness are determined by the precise range of vibrations to which they are attuned and receptive.

Life has an objective physical component which the physician, athlete, battlefield general and neuropsychologist study and act upon. But life is not defined or determined solely by the chemical and electrical events taking place in the body any more than is the creative genius of an Einstein, Ramanujan, Tesla or Beethoven reducible to neurotransmitters in their brain.

Science has discovered and deciphered marvelous secrets of physical nature through the application of the analytic mind to divide and subdivide reality into infinitesimal parts and analyze each element as if it were a separable and distinct reality. Mind artificially divides reality, and our ego separates us artificially from everyone else. The capacity for analysis has led to remarkable discoveries in science and it is a powerful tool. But as the particle physicist discovered a century ago, matter cannot be reduced to separable, independent component particles. And as the economist is discovering today, economic outcomes are not separable from political, legal, social, cultural, technological and even meteorological factors. Each individual is not separable and independent from every other individual. Each individual tunes in and gives expression to a small portion of the myriad vibrations that manifest life and consciousness transmitted holographically through the universe.

The setting forth of these premises in a handbook on new paradigm research provides a theoretical framework, and a set of hypotheses, that can be studied, tested and refined by application to the pressing political, economic, social, and ecological challenges that confront humanity in our day.

***

THE NEW PARADIGM IN MEDICINE

Health is wealth. It is our most valuable asset. Without it, we cannot live, thrive and succeed. In today's highly dynamic cultural geographies and changing industries, we are witnessing an incredible array of converging phenomena, all of which signal an urgent need for a new paradigm in the fields of health and medicine. The confluence of post-material science, technology, and health-related social movements holds out the promise of a new era of wellness not just as the absence of illness, but as an ongoing process that realizes human potential.

Ultimately the insight dawns that disease and illness have their origins in unhealed, unintegrated and unresolved psycho-emotional factors. Symptoms can be catalyzed by a gamut of experiences ranging from the psycho-spiritual and informational to the environmental. The wide-scale pollution afflicting our world today plays a significant role in triggering ill health and disease.

A new paradigm in medicine requires that we live with a more evolved consciousness. It calls for a deeper understanding of the causes of ill health and disease. Responding with solutions that serve wellness and support the aligning of body and consciousness so they function harmoniously in vibrant health is the promise of the new paradigm.

As humanity continues to explore new avenues for healing and wellness, a re-evaluation of present-day medicine and technology is taking place. The electronic, digital and wireless systems of the current paradigm prove to be causal factors in an unprecedented array of diseases. It is affecting people and animals, and the entire biosphere.

Today's wireless and digital technology is derived from sources that are detrimental and damaging to life. New solutions that support the health of living beings are already in existence, but remain virtually unknown to the general public. The alternative technologies and treatments are sourced from rich organic, mineral, and plant kingdoms and harness the energy of the Sun. They are available to nearly everyone and nearly everywhere. It is critical that we prioritize these technologies and methods if we are to bring to a halt and then reverse the devastating impact of dangerous technologies on the delicate ecosystems of the planet.

The application of the new paradigm of health and healing is still in its infancy. However, the key factors needed for a genuine paradigm shift are present. General features which mark the emergence of the new paradigm can be grouped into three main areas: 1) structural and systemic elements, 2) dynamics of social constituents and pathologies, and 3) the new knowledge that is at the core of the new paradigm emerging in science.

Systemic Elements and Social Constituents
Medical anthropology has laid out the history and politics that shape medical practice. Groundbreaking texts such as Foucault's *The Birth of the Clinic* demonstrate the level of social construction and politics involved in what is currently accepted as 'medical science' and 'clinical practice'.

Academics as well as medical professionals criticize the pharmaceutical industry, revealing that it aims to perpetuate drug manufacturing rather than the cure of patients. Alongside this practice there is the counteracting phenomenon of 'Vitamin Lawyers' who defend doctors administering curative treatments, informing them not to call their treatments drugs or cures but "vitamins." Thereby they are out of harm's way—free of the danger of being attacked by big pharma, companies that fear that effective cures will cut their profits. Paul Farmer uses the term 'structural violence.' Structural violence describes social arrangements that put individuals and populations in harm's way. He notes that "these arrangements are structural because they are embedded in the political and economic organization of contemporary societies, and they are violent because they cause injury to people."[11]

There are many lessons we can find in observing structural violence, the systemic problems of the pharmaceutical industry business model, and the highly stressful demands of hospital working conditions. The problems of the pharmaceutical industry are rooted in the materialistic understanding of illness. The "profit over people" aspect of the drug-driven business model demonstrates a lack of knowledge regarding human potential and the psychosomatic-informational understanding of human beings. The majority of drugs treat the symptoms of illnesses, the physical manifestations of disease. The application of the new paradigm in medicine shifts from symptomology to a cause-based analysis, seeking to understand the fundamental nature and cause of illness. It seeks to understand the cause of illness through various means. These include the informational-energetic origins of illness, the psycho-emotional causes of disease that manifests as illness, deficiencies and imbalances in the body, as well as

---

[11] Paul Farmer, *Pathologies of Power: Health Human Rights and the New War on the Poor.* 2005. Berkeley and Los Angeles. University of California Press.

personal lifestyle and environmental factors that cause and perpetuate illness.

The new paradigm is to analyze the cause of illness through a holistic understanding. "Information governs the processes of life in every part of the organism, and the role of information cannot be radically segmented in the organism: the information that governs the whole cannot be reduced to the information that governs the part." (The *Manifesto on the New Paradigm in Medicine*, Stresa, 2 May 2013). Disease surfacing as a cellular or organic malfunction in a part of the organism means a flaw in the information that regulates processes in the whole organism. Limitations inherent in the reductionist, mechanistic approach in medicine need to be overcome. This requires first, that we pay due attention to the curative and health-preserving potentials of natural substances. These substances are produced in and by the organism or in its life-supporting environment and are likely to contain the information needed to maintain the organism in a condition of health and vitality. We also need to observe, measure and analyze the wider interactions that maintain coherence in the organism in the context of the planet's web of life.

As opposed to current symptom-based medicine, the new paradigm is dedicated to a cause-based analysis of illness. The current paradigm views illness as a material and mechanistic process in line with classical physics, whereas the new paradigm sees illness as the manifestation of informational-energetic flows and blocks, and investigates the potential for these causes to be re-programmed through natural regenerative processes.

Re-Structuring Medical Practice

The systemic problems of today's world, together with the new paradigm emerging in the sciences, combine to reveal the need to re-define and re-structure medical practice. The new forms of medical practice aim to be more collaborative between doctor and patient. 'Health,' instead of being strictly clinical, becomes a community activity and a field of mutual learning. Some examples of this development are:

1) Paul Farmer's model of 'Teaching Hospitals'. (In a Teaching Hospital, anything that doesn't 'have to' have a doctor can have community members be trained in it. The activity of health becomes a place where doctors and patients dialogue and learn together about health and healing.

2) Community Partnerships as brought forward by public health expert Kenneth Newell in the Primary Healthcare movement. These are useful to understand how unlocking diverse forms of medical knowledge can enable a partnership between institutions and local modalities which can cut costs and make healthcare more affordable and accessible. Some examples of this are the partnering of biomedical medicine with Ayurvedic healing in India and the 'barefoot doctor' movement in China.

3) PNEI (psycho-neuro-endocrine-immunology) is a method for understanding and investigating the potentials of psychosomatic and natural cures. It also offers psychosomatic training for psychologists and psychotherapists to enable them to move beyond 'talking therapy' and develop a practice based on a more expanded consciousness.

4) Advanced methods such as *Harmonic Therapies*[12] that combine cutting-edge information-field technologies (such as TimeWaver and EPI data) with creative arts and 'Trauma-informed Practice' to directly pinpoint the informational frequencies of blockages and imbalances in the patient, and to work psychotherapeutically to resolve them.

---

[12] Siddique, Julene. *Harmonic Therapies and the Health Sciences of the Future*. Tesla Congress 2017, Belgrade.

Research in New-Paradigm Medicine

New-paradigm medicine seeks to reinforce and develop the relationship between theoretical science and medical and health-oriented practice. New-paradigm research takes medical research 'out of the clinic' and 'out of the laboratory' and engages it in the everyday world. One of the most promising aspects of the new relationship between science and medicine is demonstrated in the 'regenerative medicine' pioneered by Pier Mario Biava and Carlo Ventura in their work on re-programming information in mutant and malignant stem-cells. Their work reveals that disease, even chronic disease such as cancer, is in principle reversible.

The more we develop the new paradigm in medicine through case studies, prototypes, experiments and testing, the better grounds we have for building comprehensive systems of healthcare with updated institutions, treatments, therapies and programs. The following are some as yet open questions for research on new-paradigm medicine:

- Mapping the effect of fields on the organism:
  — The effect of the gravitational field;
  — The effect of the electromagnetic field, including electrosmog.
- Researching the function of water molecules in cells.
- Researching the electric function of the cell membrane.
- Investigating the potential of programs of treatment in information-based medicine.
- Investigating frameworks for regenerative information medicine and the reprograming of information blocks and imbalances that cause illness.
- Investigating natural cures through psycho-neuro-endocrine immunology (PNEI).

- Investigating how mental health treatments and programs can be advanced through PNEI and a psychosomatic approach.
- Investigating how the narrative of 'illness' can be re-written through narratives of regenerative medicine.
- Researching the electric model of the connection between virus and cell.
- Researching the effect of subtle energies in the environment.
- Researching the effects of high-frequency radiations (in the 100 to 1020 nm range).
- Investigating the effectiveness of traditional healing methods, including:
  - Chakra Healing;
  - Aura healing;
  - Meridian healing through acupuncture;
  - Remote healing with the aid of medical dowsing.

***

THE NEW PARADIGM IN EDUCATION

E ducation is one of the slowest of all sectors of institutional-
ized social activity to change. Yet, ironically, assumptions
and content regarding the nature of reality are changing with
alarming speed. The dominant educational system disconnects
the learner from life. The factory-style education of the past few
hundred years—where students are grouped according to age,
learning at the same pace as determined by the conveyor-belt of
course delivery, and have knowledge instilled in them through
rote memorization and regular testing—has ceased to serve the
needs of our rapidly evolving times. Graduation from this system fails to ensure the lifelong learning competencies necessary for constructive engagement with an ever-changing world.
Simultaneously, and perhaps most damaging of all, liberalism
run amok has severed education from the taproot of traditional
wisdom. Values have been relativized and discarded to a degree
unprecedented in history, breeding a nihilistic milieu in which the
very point of education—providing orientation to reality—has
been lost.

Given the technological limitations and cultural constraints
of the past, the scaling of education through the mechaniza-
tion of the educational process did previously serve the needs
of the times. But times have changed, and so have educational

technologies and paradigms. New horizons have opened and new educational systems are emerging, and the urgency of change can no longer be ignored in the institutions of education.

Re-Defining the Role of Education

The application of the new paradigm to education calls for re-defining the role as well as the process of education. This is critical both for the personal development of students, and for the acquisition and considered use of the knowledge needed for coping with the issues and problems of today's world.

The mainstream view of the function of the educational system is to offer a way for the student to "get certified," so that he or she can obtain a degree and get a job. But, more and more, research is revealing that performance in the educational setting is a poor indicator of whether the individual is equipped to deal with the requirements of life in modern society. Furthermore, the wider effects and impact of education are not adequately understood and taken into account. The new paradigm applied to education seeks to understand the effects of education in order to develop a positive role for the students in society.

The overspecialized nature of the current educational system prevents students from understanding and effectively addressing complex interconnected phenomena. One of the key benefits of the new paradigm applied to education is enabling students to see their relationship to the whole of reality—to see the bigger picture. As the premises of the new paradigm cited in this volume show, a new and comprehensible vision is emerging of our origins, our evolution, and the nature of our consciousness. The new paradigm in education can equip students to think and act with up-to-date knowledge, becoming effective agents of the change needed in the world.

In today's world information is easily accessible, and the task of education is not just to transfer information, but to develop the student's ability to analyze, discern, and apply the accessed information. Rather than memorizing and regurgitating data, the goal is to develop higher mental faculties for thinking and creativity; and to acquire capabilities for social accomplishment as well as for personal fulfillment.

The key elements of new-paradigm education (as outlined by the World University Consortium) include:

1. Development of human capacities – This refers to the shift from transmitting information to the awakening and development of the capacity to inquire, search, and think autonomously.

2. Active learning – The shift in education from listening and receiving to active learning through sharing, communicating, and co-learning with others.

3. Life-centered knowledge – The shift from emphasis placed on narrow fields of specialized knowledge to more inclusive knowledge encompassing the major dimensions of world and life.

4. Integration—The shift in emphasis from classification and analysis to synthesis and integration; from studying parts to perceiving interrelationships and interdependencies, reconciling oppositions through wider conceptual frameworks.

5. Individuality—The ability of students to integrate the knowledge accumulated by the institutions of education with the needs of society, and evolve capacities for adaptation, initiative, self-reliance, leadership, cooperation and innovation, as well as for independent thinking and creativity.

These elements of the new paradigm in education show that the learning process can be more than an instrument for "getting qualified." It can and needs to include the development of the mental and spiritual capacities of the students to acquire knowledge on their own. As pioneering thinkers such as Paulo Freire pointed out, the 'banking model' of education, where information is merely deposited, is the core of social oppression. The current educational model is far behind the needs of society, breeding only a culture of facts devoid of knowledge, and knowledge devoid of wisdom.

Wisdom was central to education in indigenous cultures, in cultures where people lived more harmoniously with each other and with nature. The new paradigm in education seeks to re-integrate the long-lost but extremely relevant element of wisdom with science-based knowledge.

Creativity is central to the new paradigm in education; it places great importance on the arts and artistic expression. For instance, how music affects cognitive development and how the arts develop and shape individual and collective identity need to be investigated and rediscovered. Long-established methods, such as Boal's Theatre of the Oppressed are among the useful tools for motivating students to ask questions about their social norms, and give them the opportunity to enact and rehearse new relationships in the context of social change. [13] In the broadest sense, new-paradigm education prepares the student to do meaningful 'work'—to beget something of evolutionary value. And doing so is rooted in the creative process.

In a world where any documented item of information can reach the fingertips of anyone connected to the Internet, the accessibility and accumulation of facts ceases to differentiate

---

[13] The Theatre of the Oppressed is a method that Augusto Boal created which uses visuals and theatrical techniques to confront oppressive behaviors. In particular, it uses forum theatre as a means of exploring isolation and oppression and of rehearsing sociopolitical change.

individuals. The new badge of education will be the ability to create, integrate, and apply knowledge grounded in deep-rooted yet perpetually refreshed wisdom. Providing the framework for acquiring, further developing and practicing such wisdom is the essential service and the lasting benefit of applying new-paradigm principles to education.

***

THE NEW PARADIGM IN POLITICS

E instein reminded us that we cannot solve the problems that confront us at the same level of thinking and consciousness that created them. Yet the current politics of nations and states reveal that nothing has changed fundamentally—we still deal with the world around us with the same level of thinking and consciousness as we did before. Not surprisingly, we still confront the same local and global problems.

We need a new paradigm in the politics of nations and states. The new paradigm must have a restorative focus: it needs to restore politics to its rightful position both in relation to economics and to society as a whole. Today, politics is seen by many as something of an anachronism, leaving economics in pride of place. In calling for a more just or greener economy, even advanced thinkers succumb to this bias. A more just and greener condition for humanity will not be delivered by devising a new form of economy alone, but by developing a new form of politics. For it is politics – regulations, taxes and redistributions – that shape an economy and impart to it a society's character and values. Politics needs to be, or to become, primary.

One reason why politics has taken a back seat is that it is *re*-active while economics and the business world to which it gave rise is *pro*-active. Economics and markets pro-actively move ahead of politics because entrepreneurial and technological innovation drive markets to expand beyond the established scale on which politics and governance operate. In doing so, the externalities that markets naturally create can no longer be managed by existing governance structures. Politics and governance are obliged to play 'catch-up'. They need to expand their scale in order to be pro-active.

Throughout history, politics has expanded in tandem with the economies it governed. When the economy expanded, politics and governance did as well. Political units moved from families to larger tribes, to city-states and on to today's "sovereign" nation-states—and regional or functional concerts of nation-states.

Our present predicament is largely due to the failure of politics to co-expand with economics, and with business. With globalization, economic markets have expanded and reached the global scale, leaving governance structures behind. As a result, many developments, from climate change to wealth inequality, are beyond the grasp of politics: they are "externalities" for the political system. Not even larger groupings of nations, such as the European Union, can cope with these processes. If the global economy is to respond to values such as sustainability and social justice, it is politics and governance, rather than economics and the economy itself that needs to be the focus of the new thinking.

A unified political voice expressed through a system of coherent, conscious and constructive conversation within the local community, escalating to the national and international level, is an instrumental necessity in new paradigm politics. The human future is fundamentally dependent on what we say, what we do, and how we do it. We need a paradigm in politics that seeks not to blame, shame or polarize, but is instead founded on creating a system of governance focused on human welfare and on the non-partisan cooperation that it calls for.

An attempt to transform politics and governance so that they operate with these aims in mind may seem fanciful. But,

as Einstein reminded us, a new paradigm always means thinking the unthinkable. Our inclination to shy away from dramatic
innovations indicates that our consciousness is as yet behind the
times. Yet we are only limited by our incapacity to understand
and mentally model political systems on a global scale. We still
operate with a consciousness that takes the nation as its primary
and often unique frame of reference.

By adopting a world-centric perspective we spot a systemic
pattern: nations are caught in a destructive vicious circle in which
they cannot escape having to competitively down-scale their
business taxes and other regulations in a never-ending bid to stay
internationally competitive. This creates a widening gap between
rich and poor nations, depressing the chances of the less privi-
leged to grow, regardless of what party and ideology is in power.

When consciousness expands to a world-centric scale, a
picture emerges that provides the vision we need to overcome
the current problems. Armed with world-centric thinking, we
see that climate change, wealth inequality, poverty, and unsus-
tainability are not the problem in themselves. Rather the problem is the narrow perspective that fuels competition between
nations without regard for the consequences on the global system
in which they operate. The whole system within which today's
nation-states operate needs to be the focus and basic reference of
the new paradigm we urgently need in politics.

***

THE NEW PARADIGM
IN ECONOMICS

T he premises of the social sciences are intended to be derived from reigning scientific premises. However, every significant premise of conventional (neoclassical) economic theory—which derives from utilitarian philosophy—is false if the premises of the new paradigm are true.

Humans as autonomic, highly individualized, hyper-rational utility-maximizing actors is a concept based on the outmoded model of Newtonian physics and its related materialist metaphysics. If taken at face value, the premises of the dominant paradigm are tantamount to a false religion. Because of this confusion and inversion of premises—the lack of realization that it is consciousness and intention that begets material outcomes rather than the other way around—the overwhelming majority of global economic activity is exploitative and noncreative. Bottom-line material outcomes are reverse-engineered into capital by taking cuts on the ever-increasing flows of money rather than ensuing from purposefully beneficial action.

Economics is designed to be a functional mapping of the economy of the real world. It follows that if the economy is changing, economics needs to change as well. However, while in the past several decades the economy has been radically changing, economics has not kept pace. It is still a patchwork of theories, methods, and working tools essentially unchanged for the last quarter of a century, without integration and updating, lacking coherence as well as relevance.

Today's economy is hallmarked by increasingly unstable financial markets, huge corporate wealth, growing capital surpluses playing the global casino in search of speculative returns, declining interest in community activity and welfare, stagnant wages, and a declining share of labor in national and regional income. There is growing inequality, increasing youth and underprivileged strata unemployment, massive corporate offshore tax evasion, and a high concentration of economic and financial power in the hands of a corporate oligarchy with mergers and acquisitions creating windfall profits. The risks of allowing this state of affairs to go unchecked are exacerbated by ecological and natural-resource constraints such as declining freshwater availability, deforestation, changes in land ownership patterns, and changes in the climate. Nonmaterial factors have assumed a dominant role, such as information, intellectual property, public trust and attitude, brand loyalty, and assumptions about biological nature and human nature. And values have become crucial elements of the evolution of the economic system as they are deciding the behavior of clients and consumers in conditions of nontransparent choices and growing complexity.

Economics, the science that maps the state of the world of production, exchange, and flow of good and services, is not keeping pace with these changes. It continues to treat society and nature as externalities rather than as basic factors in productive processes. As a result it ignores or misrepresents information regarding the social and ecological consequences of economic activity, including the economic and social cost of environmental degradation and the true cost of the replacement of nonrenewable natural resources. The dominant models are based on static equilibrium rather than the dynamics of systemic change.

They are also based on obsolete assumptions regarding the rationality of human decisions, disregarding radical shifts in values and worldviews sprouting at the periphery of society and rapidly becomingly mainstream.

These discrepancies highlight the urgent need for fundamental change in the premises of contemporary economics. The required change is not limited to a patch-up of the principal failings of economics; it requires remodeling from the ground up. The call is for a new paradigm: a paradigm that sees the economy as a network of interacting and interdependent activities oriented toward the maintenance of the human population at an acceptable level of dignity and wellbeing.

Today's economy joins 'socialized risk' with 'privatized profit'— an equation that leads to growing gaps and instability. A recent effect has been the fallout from the 2008 financial crash. As far as we can see, apart from in Iceland, no senior member of any financial institution has been imprisoned, let alone charged. Rather, the taxpayers of each affected country picked up the tab in what was euphemistically termed a "bailout" (and if the bailout was not sufficiently unjust, it was compounded by a "bail-in"—the legalized theft of the depositors' money). The global economic system has confronted the limits of the dominant paradigm and must now pivot to encompass and embrace a paradigm that contributes to human wellbeing and flourishing in a healthy, sustainable environment.

The new paradigm for mapping the world's economy has several radically new features.

— It focuses on human wellbeing rather than on material consumption and growth;
— It is creative and productive rather than consumptive and exploitative;
— It values and makes place for the engines of creativity— those sacred spaces (impervious to the assault of

numbers) where pure thought and feeling can take place and hence where real creativity can ensue;

— It seeks to move toward a real and holistic currency which redefines success by rewarding genuine worth and promotes both productivity and moral order;

— It sees human beings as the key resource in economic and social development;

— It ensures opportunities for gainful employment for all strata of the population, including the young and the elderly;

— It overseas and regulates the use of resources in view of both present and future sustainability;

— It also overseas and regulates the global casino of financial speculation that concentrates wealth in the hands of a small minority and leaves the great majority out of account;

— It encourages a fair and equitable distribution of income for people in all socioeconomic strata.

The shift to the new paradigm transforms the relationship between the economy and the environment. It brings the recognition that the economy is responsible for the quality and the sustainability of both individuals and nations, as well as for the quality and sustainability of the commons within which individuals and nations pursue the achievement of their values and objectives.

***

THE NEW PARADIGM IN BUSINESS

The role of business in the contemporary world encompasses the task of addressing the basic problems that confront the human community. Business is called upon to perform this task because it can, in principle, create prosperity for all layers of society and not just the affluent one percent, and it can also safeguard the integrity and viability of the environment. However, with the current philosophy of management, business at best tangentially reduces social harm and ecological footprint and at worst contributes to deepening socio-economic crises and environmental degradation.

The paradigm that dominates the thinking of the majority of business leaders is the heritage of the neoliberal ideology, based on classical utilitarian philosophy. It emphasizes freedom from restraints, particularly governmental restraints, and articulates the ideology of free trade and laissez-faire government. This contrasts with the meaning of the word 'liberal' often espoused in the United States, where it is characterized by social liberalism, as evidenced by civil liberties, equality, support for social justice, and endorsement of governmental regulations on questions related to inequality, welfare, healthcare, and related issues.

Neoliberalism derives from the narrative articulated in the wake of World War II by a group of economists, historians, and philosophers at the Swiss mountain retreat Mont Pèlerin. It has become so pervasive that most managers accept its assumptions without questioning or even realizing it. They take for granted that the primary goal of business is to generate financial wealth; that growth and market efficiency will lead to socially desirable outcomes; that government should be limited to border security and enforcing property rights; and that unrestrained competition and material consumerism define who people are.

Milton Friedman, one of most ardent proponents of neoliberalist business, argued that the social purpose of business, and of economic activity in general, is to maximize the wealth of the owners and shareholders. From this perspective, economic activity takes place in the context of unconstrained markets and free trade, in which an 'invisible hand' efficiently guides the allocation of resources through the decisions of self-interested, rational, utility-maximizing individuals. Globalization is an inevitable consequence of these tenets, as is inequality among people and societies.

The counterpoint to the neoliberalist paradigm is an emerging conception that sees the purpose of business as coping with the problems that beset the human community and enhancing the wellbeing of people. The new "business as service to life" paradigm is as yet virtually unknown to the mainstream of the business community. The neoliberalist paradigm with its narrative of profit maximization, free markets, and limited government intervention continues to dominate thinking in business schools, management academies, and in the marketplace. Its proponents view competition, growth, and consumerism as the defining characteristics of the world of business.

The emerging alternative paradigm recognizes that businesses are embedded in societies and in the natural environment, and that their sustenance depends on the organization and values of society as well as on the health and integrity of the environment. It acknowledges profound interconnections among people and economies, and aims for fair markets guided by responsible legislation and regulation. Ultimately, it aspires to provide the basis for institutions that work in harmony with nature rather than exploit it. However, at the mainstream of business and society, sustainability, responsibility, ethics and social justice are still seen as peripheral to the basic task of business.

Contemporary educational systems offer the opportunity to choose between the neoliberalist and the emerging business paradigm. They have the tools to maintain and transmit the ideology of business-as-usual and profit maximization, free markets, consumerism, and unfettered competition. They also dispose of the pertinent technical disciplines, functional specializations, and of the 'soft' skills relating to organizational behavior. They can espouse and transmit both the classical neoliberalist and the emerging "business as service-to-life" paradigm.

Steps are already taken in finance, agriculture, and energy, to name merely a few areas, to shift to supply chains designed for a circular economy and financial market incentives for long-term value, rather than fractional trading. Research on successful companies demonstrates the benefits of decisive paradigm change. A shift of paradigms is already in progress beyond the walls of the academic world. Companies such as Westpac Banking (Australia), IKEA (Sweden), Patagonia (USA), Schuberg Philis (Holland), Natura (Brazil) exemplify the emergence of a new kind of business model. These companies, and those that follow related practices, outperform their peers in economic terms and are distinguished by leaders and corporate cultures that embody the new paradigm.

Research on Living Asset Management Performance (the LAMP Index) confirm that companies that follow the principles of living systems are more resilient, last longer and are more financially successful than their peers. In general, companies that adopt new- paradigm thinking are

— purpose-centric and purpose-maximizing
— highly networked and decentralized, similarly to cells in the body
— regenerative in the ways they pass on their cultural DNA
— frugal in their use of energy and resources, avoiding and if possible eliminating waste
— open to feedback as a means of learning and adapting
— symbiotic in their relationships with the ecological and social systems that embed them
— conscious of both the limits and the possibilities of sustainable development in the context of the social and ecological systems in which they operate.

Questions for research

Items of research on new-paradigm business management include —

1) *Using complexity principles to leverage speed of transformation to a coherent state.* While complexity characterizes living systems, sustaining life and health relies on simple (but not oversimplified) principles. What have we learned about how to apply such principles to leading, deciding, designing, and implementing whole-system transformation?

2) *Advancing personal and organizational consciousness through immersive play to attain a purpose that exceeds the capability of any one company to achieve by itself.*

Personal and collective consciousness in the company is often below the level required to make good decisions in regard to changing conditions. Play can be effective at eliciting the growth of intelligence. How can play, using virtual, augmented, and adaptive reality, accelerate the development of consciousness in the company?

3) *Transforming large, traditionally managed companies that encounter deep-seated systemic resistance sourced in beliefs about the purpose of business.* In such companies decisions are made in alignment with beliefs recycled from the past, rather than values that design the future. Outgoing executives may be aware of the need for change but are seldom ready to embark on the journey of learning and transformation. What happens when one applies play, story-telling, and other empathy and emotion-sensitive activators to inspire transformation and remove barriers to it?

4) *Revitalizing the company spirit.* Traditional workplaces under a command and control style of management effectively numb spirit in the company into submission. Working with the three measureable indicators of company spirit (initiative, sense of control, and outlook on life), what simple acts of appreciation, support, belonging, and love could restore wholeness to the spirit that powers actions and decisions in the company?

5) *Strengthening resilience, the capacity to bounce back and leap forward through failure and adversity.* Resilience is a prerequisite of personal health as well as business

sustainability. What happens when we apply lessons learned from the Navy Seals, for instance, to transcend the challenges faced by companies and business leaders?

6) *Spreading successful initiatives to companies faced with the challenge to innovate in a resisting environment.* What inspires hope, power and strength in leaders when faced with intransigence collaborators? What principles and insights are reliable guides for effective thinking and acting under such circumstances?

* * *

PART III.
IMPLICATIONS FOR TODAY AND TOMORROW

LIVING THE NEW PARADIGM

A personal introduction

The best way to communicate 'living' something is through personal experience. Much of my life has been dedicated to trying to understand the true nature of reality—what I consider flowing balance: the dance of being and becoming in processes of emergence. My efforts have come down to understanding how emergence works through each of us—both individually and collectively—as an expression of the evolutionary dynamic of the cosmos discovered and described in the new paradigm.

Once upon a time I thought that my life quest was to learn how to dance—to dance the dance that the universe and all of creation has been dancing since time immemorial. I felt that when I observed the clouds and the birds and the herds of gazelle I could sense the beauty and the grace in the expression of life surging forward in their play of being and becoming. I longed to dance with these expressions of the cosmos, but I felt that I was constantly stepping on other people's toes, and even on my own. I wanted to dance to the rhythm of life in tune with all the expressions that flowed around and through me. I studied how birds flock, how fish school, how ungulates herd. I explored swarm phenomena and sought to differentiate between the power of collective intelligence and the drain of GroupThink. My study of traditional forms of the Martial Arts has been dedicated to this quest, and I co-founded an organization in the 1990s called Syntony Quest to center of my life aspirations.

Along the way I came to realize that it was not so much about seeking how to dance the dance of the universe, but about *being danced*. Learning how to be flowed is fundamentally different from learning how to flow. Otto Scharmer points to this difference when he seeks to describe his Theory U by quoting the violinist Miha Pogacnik. Pogacnik recounts the insight he gained from his first concert in the cathedral of Chartres:

> I felt that the cathedral almost kicked me out. 'Get out with you!' she said. For I was young and I tried to perform as I always did: by just playing my violin. But then I realized that in Chartres you actually cannot play your small violin, but you have to play the 'macro violin'. The small violin is the instrument that is in your hands. The macro-violin is the whole cathedral that surrounds you. The cathedral of Chartres is built entirely according to musical principles. Playing the macro violin requires you to listen and to play from another place, from the periphery. You have to move your listening and playing from within to beyond yourself.

In my explorations of new-paradigm evolutionary emergence in me and around me, I came to the realization that we need to engage our living experience on five levels simultaneously:

- The *intra-personal dimension* of coherence within oneself;
- The *inter-personal dimension* of coherence with one's communities and social systems;
- The *trans-species dimension* of coherence with the more-than-human world;

- The *trans-generational dimension* of coherence with past and future generations of living beings;
- The *pan-cosmic dimension* of coherence with the deep dimension of the consciousness that is immanent in the cosmos—or, in terms of the new paradigm, of the intelligence that *is* the cosmos.

By consciously, purposefully and intentionally curating each of these dimensions in dynamic relationship with the others, it may be possible for us—both personally and in the sense of our membership in the community of humanity—to live in harmony with the rhythms and dynamics of the cosmic dance of being and becoming.

Entering into authentic relation with that dance involves living and learning in the context of a community. It means learning "how to walk our talk" in the design of various forms of what I have called Evolutionary Learning Communities. It calls for combining evolutionary systems theory, social systems design methodology, and life-long-learning orientation toward individual and group self-actualization. It is to create conditions that empower individuals and groups to develop the skills necessary for the co-creation of evolutionary futures. Evolutionary learning communities are catalysts for our purposeful and creative aligning/tuning with the evolutionary processes of which we are a part.

Evolutionary systems theorist Erich Jantsch called syntony "inquiry at the evolutionary level par excellence." It involves listening to the rhythms of change and learning how to play our own melody in harmony with the larger piece. It is to seek creative aligning and tuning with the evolutionary processes of which we are a part. It is to find and create meaning and evolutionary opportunity, both individually and collectively. It is a vehicle for the cultural differentiation and purposeful orientation of social systems through convergent evolutionary pathways. Such efforts help people of all ages and walks of life to engage in consonant, coherent, and connected pathways of personal and interpersonal development, learning not only to understand, but to live the new paradigm.

***

THE NEW PARADIGM AND THE MIND OF THE NEXT GENERATION

T here is no doubt that we have entered unprecedented times. In only the past few decades we have entered the transition from national, industrial societies into the early stirrings of a planetary civilization that can be called post-historic. This new emerging epoch marks the fusion and integration of science and technologies across the physical, digital, and biological domains. It is the beginning of a completely unique ecosystem upon the planet. The First Industrial Revolution lasted roughly eighty years; the Second Industrial Revolution is generally dated as lasting around fifty; and the Third Industrial Revolution has lasted just thirty years. Within this rapidly unfolding scenario a profound uncertainty exists in how emerging technologies, the latest scientific discoveries, and new paradigm models will be adopted and developed. One thing is sure – this new unfolding revolution in human affairs will recalibrate the life of humanity upon this planet. Alongside new scientific discoveries there will also be new perspectives and models emerging in such areas as consciousness, health, business, politics, economics, education, and more. Some of these perspectives have been outlined in this brief yet articulate handbook. Alongside these new paradigm models, we will also witness a confluence of new technologies such as artificial intelligence (AI), robotics, internet of things (IoT), autonomous vehicles, 3D printing, nanotechnology, biotechnology, materials science, energy storage, and quantum computing. Never in our known human history have we been at the crossroads of such rapid and revolutionary change and transformation.

Another thing that becomes clear to us is that the next generation will be the first wave of those to be born into a globally connected and digitized world. This has never happened before to our species, and will mark the beginning of not only a new epoch upon the planet but also a new and promising phase in the future of humanity. Despite the initial 'birthing pangs' as this new global world comes into being, this marks an unprecedented era which holds great promise for our future. The new paradigms outlined in this handbook will help to lay the groundwork for a planetary civilization to emerge that will be taken up and developed by the next generation of creative, innovative, and positive-centered individuals in diverse ways. If we are to transition into an integrative, coherent phase of human civilization we need to adopt as soon as possible the new paradigm – the new map – that will then be built upon by the generations to come.

We now live in an era of global connectivity, intelligent computing, digital social media, and rapid discoveries that will shape the minds of the next generation. Some of the drivers taking us into the future are likely to be increasing global life spans that will change the nature of future generations of learners and their skill base; smart machines and automation that will significantly impact the landscape of work; computational power that will develop the Internet of Things (IoT); a new media ecology that will see technological tools shape new modes of collaboration and communication; a reorganization of our structures that will shape new means of production and value; and global connectivity that will develop new forms of diverse collaborations and integration across geographic zones. All these drivers will have significant, combined impact upon those of the next generation.

In terms of increasing global life spans the new generations will shift their approach to family life, careers, and education in light of this demographic change. Living longer, healthier lives will mean working past present retirement age, having multiple careers, and utilizing different and varied skill sets rather than one career path. This will make them lifelong learners, open and adaptable to new skills and opportunities. The next generation will also be the first to be born into an age of smart machines where they will naturally find themselves living and working alongside 'deep learning' machines and smart infrastructure. These will be increasingly commonplace in our offices, factories, and homes. Smart machines will become an integral part of our education, health, security, production, and service provider lifestyles. Living with such smart infrastructures will seem the norm to the next generation, and they will feel comfortable in collaborating and co-depending upon them. It will also force the mind of the next generation to focus on the skills that are uniquely human. Rather than dehumanizing us, such smart environments are likely to refocus our thinking upon the skills, assets, and inherent abilities that make us human. The next generation will find themselves living in a world of incredible computational power where almost all interactions will be with a world full of information, data, and communication. They will form new relationships with software, such as AI agents, that today some of us may feel cautious about. Yet when being born into such a world it will feel natural to form relations and alliances with forms of smart software that will assist and complement our human lives.

A new media ecology will continue to develop upon the current platforms that will transform the way all young people will communicate, produce, and share their thinking and creativity. This media ecosystem will consist of social media, video production, gaming platforms, augmented reality, and citizen journalism. This ecology, which is ushering in a new form of communicative language, will explore transparency and will be a critical eye upon social, political, and cultural behavior. Young people especially will be strong media content generators, offering innovative projects as well as producing multimedia commentary upon social events. They will become a powerful new wave of citizen journalism that will penetrate beyond the hypocrisy often provided by mainstream news outlets. A strong online presence in this new media ecology will place demands on, and thus also develop, cognitive and attention skills relative to these collaborative platforms. These developing social media platforms will be indicative of how structures and organizations are moving away from the older hierarchical top-down forms and into decentralized and distributed relations. This will affect how the new generations interact and communicate both at local as well as global levels.

The next generation will also be the first generation to be born into an emerging planetary civilization. For them the world will seem globally connected across national and state borders, bringing together a wealth of diversity, creativity, innovation, and collaborative potentials. It will also change how personal relations are formed, and 'distant,' diverse relationships will become more the norm as the next generation are likely to consider themselves as global citizens first and foremost. The notion of 'distant' relationships will not have the same meaning as they do today, as global technologies will continue to contract the sense and meaning of space and time. The mind of the next generation will feel instantly connected to people from all areas of the world, and are likely to be in constant communication through 'real-time' technologies. Already psychologists are recognizing the rise of empathy amongst many of the younger generation as these youngsters are able to relate to people, often strangers, across the globe that are in difficulties or experience challenging times. This sense of human solidarity, a feeling of compassion for others, is likely to be stronger within the minds and hearts of the next generation as they feel naturally connected to those from beyond their localized communities.

These future drivers are set to usher in a new paradigm in terms of how as a human community we live, connect, communicate, collaborate, understand, produce, and create value and meaning in our lives. These changes across our diverse cultures and societies will influence and shape the new minds of the generations to come. In this way, the minds of the next generation will naturally exhibit new skill sets and ways of thinking. These are likely to include skills of social intelligence, sense-making, adaptive thinking, cross-cultural awareness, new media literacy, and a visual perspective.

Social intelligence implies an ability to connect deeply with others, both in physical and digital relations, and especially in extended networks, which will be more highly developed in the next generation. The next generation will be more aware and sensitive to interactions across national, ethnic, and cultural groups. Due to the nature of living in an interconnected world, new sets of social skills will be required that will demand a sensitive understanding to diversity and difference. The new paradigm is about embracing this diversity whilst seeking balance, harmony, and unity. This greater awareness will assist the next generation in cultivating how they make sense ('sense-making') of the world. That is, having the ability to intuit the deeper meanings and significances in what is being expressed; sometimes this will mean understanding beyond the language used. Making sense not only of our environment but also of the meaning behind words, expressions, and social behavior is one of the features that make us human. The next generations, as part of an emerging planetary civilization, are likely to cultivate and manifest to a high degree this sense-making as part of their daily lives.

As a complement to sense-making, adaptive thinking is also likely to be a feature of the new paradigm, as new models and perspectives will be needed to examine and tackle many of the issues we will continue to be faced with in the world. Old rules and ways of thinking will no longer apply as the world undergoes a radical shift in its systems and old-paradigm models. This broad-based integral thinking will be an essential part in developing cross-cultural awareness. This is sometimes referred to in psychological terms as 'situational awareness' or 'situational adaptability.' This will prove to be an important skill for the next generation as they will find that the only genuine way to create progress in the world will be through cross-cultural dialogue and collaboration. The new paradigm is about embracing holistic, integral, whole thinking and behavior that transcends linear patterns.

As part of the emerging 'always-on' digitally connected world the next generation will naturally learn new forms of media literacy that will see them participating across a range of multiple platforms. The next generation of young people will need to gain fluency in not only online social platforms but also in content-production. This may include the creation of their own video/media as communication continues to become highly visual in our digital cultures. The future is likely to become more visually orientated, especially as tools and practices of augmented reality become more common. Virtual reality environments for meetings and collaborations will also become more prevalent. In this way, the minds of the next generation are likely, through cultural stimuli, to become more highly developed in the visual, and hence right-brain, perspective.

In summary, we have entered the beginnings of a new era where we can expect great changes throughout our varied socio-cultural systems – health, business, politics, economics, education, consciousness, and more. The Laszlo Institute of New Paradigm

Research attempts to map and explore these shifts and to seek ways to navigate the transformations ahead. This Handbook is a reflection of the work of the Institute, and it is hoped that its research and explorations will assist those of the next generation, to whom we shall collectively be passing on our legacy. Of course, the future is never guaranteed, and both unpleasant disruptions as well as 'disruptive innovations' are often part of the complex unfolding of paradigms. Whilst it is likely that further disturbances and difficulties are to be experienced, the future still holds great promise and potential as long as humanity can accept to pass the baton to the next generation.

The mind of the next generation is going to be rewired for a different world. The young people who will next take up the mantle for advancing change upon this planet will express themselves in a way that will embrace what we call the new paradigm. Theirs promises to be an exciting world full of possibility, potential, and opportunity. It will also be a time for courage, self-belief, and self-lessness. It promises to be a remarkable future that is awaiting tomorrow the young people of today.

***

CURRENT PROJECTS OF THE INSTITUTE

Project *Conscious World*

The prevailing orientation to reality—consumptive, short-term, 'numbers-maximizing'—has led to dangerous and unsustainable imbalances at the individual, societal and planetary levels. Yet there is evidence that the world is already changing. A different paradigm is rapidly emerging premised on a more highly "conscious," "mindful," and "spiritual" civilization. *Project Conscious World* seeks to exhibit, celebrate and encourage the achievements at the vanguard of both 21st century science and spiritual development. It will:

- Create a vision of an alternative future based on actual, inspirational examples from all domains of modern human civilization in which visionary leaders have already begun to embed "conscious"/"mindful"/"spiritual" processes and practices;
- Create a set of powerful resources, learnings, and tools to accelerate such change;
- Build communities of leaders in a variety of key areas (such as education, media, public health, business, etc.) to work together to embed such change in their respective fields.

LEVEL 1: The evolution toward a conscious world is depicted as an interactive multimedia honeycomb, with each cell representing a distinct human discipline. The honeycomb will be populated with ever-increasing numbers of relevant case studies—initially by the project team with the expectation that others, through an open platform, would populate thousands of further cells via peer-to-peer engagement [beginning with case studies in the education field]. Post 'site launch', any site visitor could open up a cell and populate the given web page, which will be curated to ensure quality.

LEVEL 2: Learnings/resources/best practices will be synthesized from the case studies in Level 1 and distilled into a "Consciousness Library" (for use by aspiring organizations)

LEVEL 3: Communities of transformation will be catalyzed to embed conscious processes throughout distinct spheres of civilization (e.g., business, education, health, etc.)

LEVEL 4: Various kindred technology-enabled spiritual tools and movements will be partnered with and publicized/ virally disseminated through the web portal.

The first phase of the project focuses on the 'Education Cell' of the 'honeycomb'. This shall be the first cell to be populated as we identify, organize, and analyze developments occurring globally in the field of Conscious Education and synthesize and distill "education best practices."

Project *WorldShift*

WorldShift (WS) will serve as an active global initiative in service of peace, sustainability, restorative justice, compassionate action, and conscious communication. Humanity is moving through an unprecedented window of time that affords a rare opportunity to facilitate a shift in consciousness and catalyze enlightened action for and on behalf of humanity. Populated by an international community of new-paradigm visionaries, conservationists,

ecologists, environmentalists, scientists, humanitarians, philosophers, inventors, writers, artists and conscious evolutionists, WS
will seek to initiate, co-create and campaign for evolutionary
progress and global transformation.
WS will promote and support the establishment of global unity
and harmony culturally, socio-politically, environmentally, eco-
logically, economically and spiritually. It is committed to the
co-creation of the new paradigm and throiugh it to the establishment of a peaceful and harmonious and world.

**The Collaborative Kyung Hee University *Global Shift Leader-
ship* Module**
Current research is being carried out through a collaborative
alliance between Kyung Hee University in South Korea and the
Laszlo Institute of New Paradigm Research. Groundwork is being
laid for the establishment of a "GlobalShift Leadership Program"
with a research agenda dedicated to the emergence of a new paradigm in education. The Program brings together a multi-cultural
research team to curate the emergence of educational models,
methods, curricula and delivery platforms that both reflect the
emerging vision and at the same time meet the needs of a new
generation of learners faced with the challenge of coping with the
local and global problems of our times. If the Program is successful, it will be offered to various universities worldwide.

Projects in Development
Neuroendocrine Fatigue (also known as myalgic encephalo-
myelitis or 'chronic fatigue syndrome'), a project focussed on
research on this little-understood health condition. It is to explore
whether the symptoms of fatigue are the result of various organ
systems entering into altered, abnormal states intentionally, as a
self-protective equilibrating mechanism. Research is to explore
the possibility that no conventional disease process is at work,

with the body's abnormal and 'entangled' responses being functionally oriented to help restore homeostasis. If the hypothesis is validated by further research and experimentation, the possibilities of a practical recovery program will be investigated.

Effect of trees and natural environments on the human cellular system, a project to explore how the biosphere impacts on the quality of human lives. Studies are to focus on the relevance of green spaces for mental, physical, social and behavioral health, starting from the general 'system' of human habitat-associated gardens, parks, and forests. Other, related research is to center on the change of ionization in green spaces, and on exploring how to measure and produce further negative ions with outdoor and indoor plants.

***

PUBLICATIONS OF THE INSTITUTE

Book Series
The New Paradigm Books of the Laszlo Institute
Published by Select Books, New York

> *What Is Consciousness*, Ervin Laszlo, Jean Houston, Larry Dossey, 2016
> *What Is Reality*, Ervin Laszlo with Alexander Laszlo, 2016
> *The Laszlo Chronicle*, Gyorgyi Szabo, 2017
> *What Is the New Paradigm*, ed. Kingsley Dennis, 2018
> The *Tuscany Dialogues*, Ervin Laszlo and Michael Tobias, 2018

Periodical
WORLD FUTURES: The Journal of New Paradigm Research
Published by Routledge, Taylor & Francis Group, Philadelphia and London
(as of Volume 70, 2014)

BIOGRAPHIES OF THE CO-AUTHORS

Lawrence Bloom ["The New Paradigm in Economics"] is currently Secretary General of the Be Earth Foundation, a UN Inter Government Organization combining creative financial and technical solutions enabling countries, corporations and sovereign wealth funds to achieve their sustainable development goals and targets. He is also Chairman of the Dakia Institute and Be Energy Group. He was recently voted by SALT magazine as among the top 25 most Conscious Global Leaders, and has received an award at the UN from the Humanitarian Innovation Forum for Conscious Leadership. Formerly, Lawrence managed the International Hotel Group's $3B global real estate portfolio. Lawrence was appointed the first Chairman of the World Economic Forum at Davos, Global Agenda Council on Urban Management and is also a former Chairman of the UN Green Economy Initiative, Green Cities, Buildings and Transport Council.

John Bunzl ["The New Paradigm in Politics"] is a global political activist and businessman and founder of the Simultaneous Policy (Simpol) campaign, a means for removing the barriers which prevent many of today's global problems from being solved. Simpol has since steadily been gathering increasing attention, recognition and support amongst citizens, activists, non-governmental organizations, politicians, business people and many others. He has authored or co-authored many books, the latest being *The Simpol Solution – solving global problems could be easier than we think,* co-authored with Nick Duffell. He has lectured widely, including to The Schumacher Society, The World Trade Organization, The Lucis Trust and at various universities around the world.

Nicolya Christi ["The New Paradigm in Medicine", "The New Paradigm in Politics", "WORLDSHIFT"] is a futurist and author. Her first book 2012: *A Clarion Call: Your Soul's Purpose in Conscious Evolution* was placed in the top ten of Spring 2011 book reviews by Publishers Weekly. She has a background training in humanistic and transpersonal psychotherapy (Psychosynthesis and Core Process) and various nonviolent communication practices, and has developed several psycho-spiritual maps and models for evolving consciousness to bring new paradigm dimensions to psychological and spiritual understanding.

Kingsley L. Dennis, PhD, ["The New Paradigm and the Mind of the Next Generation"] writer and researcher, is Publications Director of the Laszlo Institute and is the author of several critically acclaimed books including *The Phoenix Generation, New Consciousness for a New World, Struggle for Your Mind, After the Car,* and the celebrated *Dawn of the Akashic Age* (with Ervin Laszlo). His book *The Sacred Revival* was published in 2017. He also created the self-publishing imprint "Beautiful Traitor Books" and is writing books also for the children's market. His most recent book is *Sophie's Search for No-Where* (June 2017). Born in the UK, he currently lives in Andalusia, Spain.

Shamik Desai [Part II "Introduction"; "The New Paradigm in Education"; "ConsciousWorld"] is Executive Director of the Laszlo Institute and worked with the Institute's Director in editing the present Handbook. He grew up in San Francisco, studying economics at Stanford University with a term at Oxford. He worked as a banker at various institutions, including Morgan Stanley in New York, Cisco Systems in the Silicon Valley, and the World Bank in Washington, DC. Subsequently he pursued a master's degree in international public policy with a focus on political philosophy at Johns Hopkins University. His satirical-philosophical novel about modern capitalists migrating to a 'currency of consciousness' domain inspired a social giving app that encourages and measures people's giving attitudes.

Garry Jacobs Ph.D. ["Application of the New Paradigm to the Sciences of Life"] is an American writer, researcher and consultant on the topics of business management, economic and social development, and global governance. He is CEO of the World Academy of Art & Science; Chairman of the Board and CEO of the World University Consortium; Managing Editor of the journal *Cadmus*; Vice-President of The Mother's Service Society; Distinguished Professor of Interdisciplinary Studies at the Person-Centered Approach Institute, Italy; Executive Director of the International Center for Peace and Development in Napa, California; and a member of the Club of Rome.

Dawna Jones ["The New Paradigm in Business"] is a Canadian writer and global change-agent, founder of www.frominsight toaction.com, and author of Decision Making for Dummies. She served for eight years as host of the Evolutionary Provocateur podcast and currently hosts the Insight to Action podcast for business innovators. Her mission is to accelerate the growth of consciousness through the spiritual technology she gained from years of experience with energetic sensitivity. She applies new technologies, such as Virtual Reality, to accelerate the evolution of new-paradigm thinking in the business world.

Alexander Laszlo, Ph.D. ["The New Paradigm in Education" and "Living the New Paradigm"], is Director of the Doctoral Program in Leadership and Systemic Innovation at the Buenos Aires Institute of Technology (ITBA), and served as the 57th President as well as Chair of the Board of Trustees of the International Society for the Systems Sciences. He has worked for UNESCO, the Italian Electric Power Agency, and has been named a Level I Member of the National Research Academy of Mexico (SNI). He is the author of more than eighty-five journal, book, and encyclopedia publications and serves on the Editorial Board of six internationally arbitered research journals. He is the recipient of the Gertrude Albert Heller Award, the Sir Geoffrey Vickers Memorial Award, and the *Förderpreis Akademischer Klub* award.

Christopher Laszlo, PhD, ["The New Paradigm in Business"] is the Char and Chuck Fowler Professor of Organizational Behavior, and Executive Director of the Fowler Center for Business as an Agent of World Benefit, at Case Western Reserve University. He is the author of Flourishing Enterprise: The New Spirit of Business (2014), Embedded Sustainability: The Next Big Competitive Advantage (2011), Sustainable Value: How the World's Leading Companies are Doing Well by Doing Good (2008) and The Sustainable Company (2003). He serves as general editor of the second volume of the Encyclopedia of Sustainability (2010) and Fellow of the International Academy of Management. In 2012, he was selected one of the "Top 100 Thought Leaders" in conscious business. In 2015, he was elected to the International Academy of Management.

Ervin Laszlo, Doctorat d'Etat Sorbonne ["Part I"] is Founder and Director of the Laszlo Institute, Founder and President of The Club of Budapest, Fellow of the World Academy of Arts and Sciences, Member of the Hungarian Academy of Science, the International Academy of Philosophy of Science, Senator of the International Medici Academy, and Editor of the international periodical *World Futures: The Journal of New Paradigm Research.* He is the recipient of the Goi Peace Prize (2002), the International Mandir of Peace Prize (2005), the Conacreis Holistic Culture Prize (2009), the Ethics Prize of Milano (2014), the Luxembourg Peace Prize (2017) and was nominated for the Nobel Peace Prize in 2004 and 2005. He holds Honorary PhD's from the United States, Canada, Finland, and Hungary and is the author or co-author of fifty-four books translated into twenty-four languages.

Maria Sagi Ph.D. ["The New Paradigm in Medicine"] is a native of Budapest. She began her career as a classical pianist and turned subsequently to the study of medicine and psychology, specializing in personality theory, deep psychology, social psychology and the psychology of music. She received her Ph.D. in psychology at the Eötvös Lóránd Science University of Budapest, and her C.Sc. (Candidate of the Hungarian Academy of Sciences) following seven years of research. Former Research Associate and Scientific Secretary of the Institute for Culture and Sociological Research of the Hungarian Academy of Sciences, Dr. Sági is the author or co-author of eleven books and hundred and fifty articles and research papers. She currently serves as Science Director of the Club of Budapest.

Julene Siddique MA, MMus. ["The New Paradigm in Medicine" and "The New Paradigm in Education"] is a Composer, Academic, and Therapist. She is the Composer, author of The Odyssey Musical Theatre premiering in 2018. She has both researched and worked extensively on the intersections between the Arts, Health and Culture, and is founder of the "Spectrum" method

of education which integrates personal and professional development. She is currently creating a new paradigm framework for
"Social Philosophical Science" to engage individual as well as collective forms of transformation.

***

THE LASZLO INSTITUTE OF NEW PARADIGM RESEARCH

Villa Demidoff, 1 Avenue Demidoff, Bridge Seraglio,
55022 Bagni di Lucca (LU) Italy
www.laszloinstitute.com

www.ingramcontent.com/pod-product-compliance
Lightning Source LLC
Chambersburg PA
CBHW050546280326
41933CB00011B/1738